How to Develop
a Praying Church

How to Develop
a Praying Church

Charlie W. Shedd

♪

ABINGDON PRESS
Nashville   New York

HOW TO DEVELOP A PRAYING CHURCH

Copyright © 1964 by Abingdon Press

ISBN 0-687-17773-1

Library of Congress Catalog Card Number: 64-15761

SET UP, PRINTED, AND BOUND BY THE
PARTHENON   PRESS,   AT   NASHVILLE,
TENNESSEE, UNITED STATES OF AMERICA

DEDICATION

To the more than
five hundred people in
Memorial Drive Presbyterian
Church, Houston, Texas, who
have covenanted with God to
daily prayer for their fellow
members and for others
outside the church

Contents

    I. "My House Shall Be Called
           a House of Prayer" 9

   II. Foundations for Prayer 18

  III. Call to Disciplined Living 28

  IV. The Undershepherds 40

   V. The Undershepherds at Work 51

  VI. The Prayer Chains 66

 VII. Youth at Prayer 80

VIII. Growing in Prayer 94

        Tested Bibliography 109

"The Church will win the world for Christ when—and only when— she works through living spirits steeped in prayer."

EVELYN UNDERHILL
Light of Christ

Chapter I

"My House Shall Be Called
a House of Prayer"

A THRILLING NEW DEVELOPMENT IS underway in the Christian church of our generation. Denominationally and individually we are hearing from many sources a sincere reecho of the disciples' plea, "Lord, teach us to pray!"

We can be deeply grateful for this emerging sign of new life. Sharp criticism of the church from within the church itself calls our attention to the fact that we are a long way from what Christ had in mind for us.

John Heuss in his cryptic article "The True Function of the Christian Church" joins many other writers of our day as he reminds us:

We all need to get a clear grasp again on what the Spirit-filled fellowship, which came into existence immediately after Pentecost, was like. What it did to people, your parish and mine should be doing to people now. Its peculiar

9

qualities should be the qualities that distinguish our parishes from the world around us. . . . Its motivating spiritual dynamics should drive and dominate us. We should take it as our model and be sharply critical of anything in our parish life which does not conform to its predominant characteristics.

He says it well. It is imperative that we continually judge our accomplishments by standards spelled out from the mind of Christ. And any group of people which sets itself to discover their Lord's most specific direction to his church will ponder long before his quotation in the temple: *"My house shall be called a house of prayer"* (Matt. 21:13, Mark 11:17, and Luke 19:46).

It might be argued whether this was Jesus' most specific expression of his desire for his church. But serious students of the Word will hold it for prime consideration.

Yet most of us in the church will confess that too often we have busied ourselves at countless other points in our development. The mighty preacher, Thomas Chalmers, was once pondering over why, in spite of all his efforts and enormous popularity, there was not more spiritual outcome to show for it all. He came to this conclusion—he was trusting his "own animal heat and activity" rather than the Holy Spirit.

Many a perspiring clergyman bows in humility before this charge. So does his church.

10

Most of us suspect sometimes that we are over-heavy with plans and promotion, overconcerned with policy and print, overindulged with patronage and pleasure. So, since we must do something, we whip up new clubs and devise ingenious sharp approaches. We initiate appeals and drives and funds and movements. We pump new wind through the bellows hoping that the whole organ will give off more noble sounds through all our doing.

Yet when we quiet ourselves in our wheeling and dealing, we sometimes hear what seems like groaning. Is this the Spirit of God tuning us in to the weary shuffle of nonspiritual programs in his church? Is this the soul of Christ crying again, "My house shall be called a house of prayer"?

Question: Why is the church unable to influence society at the points where it needs Christ most? Can it be that we have been giving our energies to the wrong things? Have we so concerned ourselves with good works *for* God that we have too little left for communion *with* God?

If we are sensitive to this false alignment of our efforts, we will take courage from the sure signs of a growing new interest in prayer. The word "new" must be properly interpreted if it is to be used in this connection. Things "new" to us may have long roots from the past.

Careful observers of the early church point out that the first followers of Christ wasted no time in obeying his directives. Early records of their activity include this vivid description: "They devoted themselves to the apostles' teaching and fellowship, to the breaking of bread and prayers" (Acts 2:42).

The student of Christian history knows that the church in its early life *was* these small groups who gathered to share with one another the intimate things stirred up by the Holy Spirit in their hearts.

At first there were no budget drives, no men's clubs, no mimeograph machines. There were no board meetings nor mission boards. Organs and organizations; files and figures; pews, pastors, and phones; program, pomp, and pageantry—these were yet to come.

There was nothing here but the Lord Jesus and a few deeply dedicated disciples gathered to warm their hearts by his Risen Presence. They were come together to be taught of him, to share his love with one another, and to be used however he saw fit. They gathered in back rooms and upper chambers, in boats, and on hillsides to pray, to study, and to receive their orders for the establishment of his Kingdom.

In New Testament times to be a Christian was to belong to a fellowship of believers who had big things to accomplish and needed one another's support to get them done. But more than this they needed the common life centered in Christ. They banded together to talk about him, to listen to his

12

Spirit speak to them, to read from the Scripture, to ponder the letters of their leaders, and to eat together the bread of communion at his table. He said he would come when two or three of them gathered together in his name. They believed his promise and felt his Presence.

In the centuries which followed, again and again this same pattern of power repeated itself. Close observation of the church in the Middle Ages finds certain men of spiritual dynamics gathering small companies to themselves for prayer and study, training and service. When the church became corrupt of clergy and ceremonially bogged down, even then there were little units of "the real church" sharing the fellowship of the Holy Spirit. Sometimes it seems to the careful student that these groups alone were the single healthy factor in a decaying ecclesiasticism. Such orders as "the Franciscans" kept alive a spark of spiritual glow in the dying fires of Romanism.

It has been like that in every age. The early Religious Society of Friends came into being when men like George Fox were determined to be "children of light" in a day of darkness. In the togetherness of silence this reforming nucleus of Quakers waited on the Lord and felt the quickening power of the Inner Presence in a manner which brought fresh energy to the whole church.

13

In the eighteenth century four students at Oxford University began the famous Wesleyan revival of Methodism. They committed themselves to the study of Scripture, to visit prisons, to stir up spiritual conversations wherever they found an opening, and to live the Christ-disciplined life both collectively and personally.

The continuing success of the Methodist movement both in England and America was the "class meeting" of ten members who often came together for nurture and direction. Here "regular folks" and the socially elite found fellowship. Here the wretched and the outcast found hope. Here the Spirit transformed lives and brought spiritual awakening to a society which was hung on the dead centers of inertia and sin.

Almost thirty years ago in many parts of Christendom there arose a "new" prayer interest which bids fair to become a major factor in the modern church. It seemed to rise spontaneously from many origins. One of its leaders estimates that there are currently ten thousand separate small units meeting regularly in our land for study and prayer.

Today fellowships of this type are to be found in factories and offices, colleges and universities, downtown restaurants and suburban homes. Within the church and outside the church, men and women are exploring together the deep things of the spirit and seeking divine guidance for this generation.

14

Dozens of churches in Protestantism are calling their people to participate in this "new" movement. The witness of ministers and leaders who are fortunate enough to work with these is most encouraging. They testify that such groups have an amazing ministry to those who take them seriously. Homes are saved, attitudes changed, old problems resolved, unhealthy emotions healed, and new dimensions of soul reached when people dedicate themselves to a life of prayer.

The testimony of Scripture, the teaching of history, and the witness of moderns make this very clear: spiritual renaissance does come to the church whenever a nucleus responds to Christ in depth and when they do this together in intimate fellowship. In the Bible, in generations past, and in our midst now the Holy Spirit works with revolutionary power when small companies of Christians wait on him.

Memorial Drive Presbyterian Church of Houston, Texas, is one of the many new congregations which have sprung up on America's urban landscape.

There has been considerable crying in these latter days that the church is moving to the suburbs and isn't that too bad? It is too bad if the inner city is left without the ministry of Christ. Yet the suburban church need not be just a feeble reflection of modern suburbia. It should and can be a powerful force; for suburbia is where the people are going and those of us who are working in this area ought to see it as a fresh new challenge in American Protestantism.

The new mobility of Americans is not all bad. Could it be that the Holy Spirit himself has stirred up his ancient landmarks because he can do more with his people in new settings? If we listen well to his direction he may give us fresh insights and dynamic new approaches which can redound to his glory.

When the new Houston congregation began seven years ago, a handful of serious churchmen asked themselves, "What does Christ want this church to be?" Questions on the agenda included, "What things in your last church would you care to see carried over into this church?" "What would you like to do different here?" "If you could draw a word picture of this church twenty years from now, what would you include?"

As these suburban minds struggled before such questions, three major conclusions began to emerge:

1. They would develop an intense training program for officers and leaders and a serious instruction course for the education of members.

2. They would take on a benevolence program which called for genuine sacrifice and required them to continually lift their eyes beyond the horizons of their own parish.

3. They would strive to become a "house of

prayer" in keeping with Jesus' statement of Matt. 21:13.

This book is a report of the experiments in prayer which have developed from point three. Today in the work described on these pages there are more than five hundred people who have made a prayer covenant with God and their church leaders. Two hundred and fifty of these serve as Undershepherds who, by specific assignment, have pledged themselves to pray for certain of their fellow members. (See Chaps. IV and V.) Seventy high school young people and nearly one hundred additional adults comprise the prayer chain workers. (See Chap. VI.) The remainder pray daily through the disciplines of prayer groups and through other programs designed to bring as many as possible into a fellowship of prayer.

It will be readily apparent that this is no panacea for the ills of the church. We have not arrived at some utopia where all is exactly as it should be in a local parish. The true "house of prayer" is still only a goal toward which we move. We know some things which do not work for us and others which seem to bear the stamp of the authentic. From the things we have learned, we present here a report which we hope may be helpful to others interested in the "new" movements of prayer life within the Protestant church.

Chapter II

Foundations for Prayer

WHEN FIVE HUNDRED PEOPLE PRAY daily by a special covenant, it is important that they (a) understand what they are doing and (b) have a sound theological platform from which to pray.

This book does not purpose to be a treatise on the theology of prayer. There are many excellent works which deal adequately with the underlying doctrines of this theme. But the reader may wish to know some of the basic precepts which we teach our people as they seek to create a "house of prayer" in this church. A brief summary of each precept is presented here as background for our experiment in the development of a praying church.

I

Prayer is for discovering God's will. We do not pray in order that we might get what we want. Prayer is for finding out what God wants from us.

We pray in order that we might become instruments for his glory.

Who can escape personal indictment from that so-human movement when James and John came to Jesus saying, "Master, we would that thou shouldest do for us whatsoever we shall desire" (Mark 10:35)?

Most of us do not point an accusing finger. They were reflecting the natural tendency of man to ask of all propositions, "What will this do for me?" But Jesus, in his usual incisive fashion, reversed their thinking and told them that his kind of religion was for people who were prepared to do something for God. Always he taught that God is not an eternal blessing machine for men but that men are to be instruments for the blessing of God.

This point is placed first here, not because it is number one in importance, but because it meets most people where they are when they begin thinking of prayer. Whether the church has mistakenly taught this, or whether modern man has picked it up elsewhere, the fact stands that most people's first thoughts of prayer are heavy with "give *me,*" "help *me,*" "do this for *me.*" Even when we are alert to this truth we often catch ourselves trumping up our own wishes into the business of God.

The true praying church will hear often ringing through its halls the call of "surrender," "commitment," "self-renunciation." Have we been so

19

anxious for people to ''join up'' that we have failed to emphasize the ''centering down'' which is a major part of the full gospel?

That person who earnestly prays will come soon to this inescapable fact: The art of prayer is not learning how to switch God's goodness onto our little track. It is rather the art of turning our little engines onto the rails of the Lord whose road leads us by his route to his Kingdom.

Our Heavenly Father wants us to experience the fullness of his love. But he does not offer it to us on our terms. If we are to know the power of the Resurrection, we must know the agony of the Crucifixion by which sin dies in us. Christ gave himself absolutely, with no strings attached. So also must we. Prayer is a call for the abandonment of our will to the divine Will.

II

The first move of prayer is God's move. We do not initiate the divine-human encounter. Prayer is not the business of finding God. It is rather a matter of being found by the God who made man for himself.

We frequently call attention to biblical definitions of prayer in training our prayer workers. Chief among these is what we call ''the Bible's perfect definition of perfect prayer.'' It is Rev. 3:20:

"Behold, I stand at the door, and knock: if any man hear my voice, and open the door, I will come in to him."

This is what prayer is *first*. By his very nature God moves in at any heart door where he hears the sincere petition, "Come in!"

The true student of prayer would never say that frantic beating at God's doors is not prayer. Any crying of the heart to its Creator is prayer, of a sort. But the inmost secrets of prayer are reserved for those who understand that prayer is neither hunting God down, nor storming his gates, nor pleading with him for his presence. Real prayer is the quiet opening of doors, conscious and subconscious; doors easily opened and doors which creak on rusty hinges; doors which gladly fling wide and doors with embarrassment written large on their name plates; doors of the mind, body, soul. Christian prayer is opening up to the Lord, who knocks and waits and longs to come in.

We teach our people that they do not need to badger an unwilling Heavenly Father into being nice to his children. God longs to love and to nourish, to judge and refine, to add to and take away from, to destroy what should be destroyed, and to save what is his own. Prayer is communion with the Lord. It is a constant friendship, a thrilling relationship to the One who comes to seek, to save, and to bless.

In the instructions to our Undershepherds and prayer chain members, in our work with prayer groups and those who have assumed the intercessory responsibilities of our church, we have two simple "starter" points for all beginners.

The first of these is the innocent-looking reminder: *begin your prayers with God.*

But this is not so natural as it may sound. When we pray about an ache in our back, most of us are prone to begin with our aching back. Yet effective praying about any problem does not start with the problem and seek to bring God down to it. Those who know tell us that we pray right only when we begin with God and bring our problems to him. If Mary is our intercessory responsibility, our work is not to bring God to Mary but Mary to God.

This is why the mystics and the saints of prayer place so much emphasis on adoration. This is why Jesus began his great teaching on prayer with the opening phrase, "Our Father which art in heaven, Hallowed be thy name!" Students of the Lord's Prayer rightly point out that the prayer is halfway done before we even begin to talk of our needs. The first petitions of our Lord's Prayer are not man-askings but God-askings.

Because God is already acting in this relationship, our first movement in prayer is *response* not request. It is loving him back because he first loved us.

22

III

A third prayer precept which receives major emphasis in our training is summed up in the other "starter" point for all beginners: *Pray in your own way! There are twelve gates into the holy city and a thousand different doors to prayer. When we pray we are entering a vast expanse of truth which leaves room for much experiment and many approaches.*

Anyone who prays much will feel a warm kinship with the Brittany fisherman's prayer as he puts out to sea in the morning: "O Lord keep me, for the sea is so big and my boat is so little!"

Now and then in any praying church there comes on scene someone whose approach smacks large with: "If only you prayed like I pray, then you would really pray!" We work with these and hope that they may one day become more flexible. But if they are allowed to go unchecked, they may have a damaging effect on the neophyte who doesn't know how and knows that he doesn't know.

Jesus said, "Other sheep I have, which are not of this fold," and it is a mistake to assume that we have an option on truth. We must allow for revelation in unexpected places. This is why we do not draw a tight line around early training. It is our conclusion that some people pray naturally in ways peculiar to themselves. Others must struggle before they develop their own effectiveness. For this reason we keep constantly repeating the point, "Pray in your own way!"

We will long remember that night in our early development when the Undershepherds were meeting to discuss their work. During the witness moments a young car salesman said, "I'm doing just fine, thank you, and I don't want to talk about it. My system works for me, and I don't think I could describe it so you'd understand. But I feel good about it, and I think I'm getting through. So if you don't mind I'll pass."

He taught us something important that night. No human knows all there is to know about prayer. There are no experts in this domain. Only God knows what is good and we best allow plenty of room for individual growth. We tell our starters and often remind our veterans that prayer is a personal matter. We only ask that each person in this work be sincere in his efforts, serious in his own education, and prepared to share *when he is ready* whatever he thinks may be helpful to the whole.

Although it may appear that this particular point is not theological, we believe it stems from an important doctrinal base. Worship is partly wonder, and the true adoration of God calls for a humble spirit which knows that God's thoughts are far greater than our thoughts and his ways far above our ways. For this reason we teach our praying people to linger long in meditation before such verses

24

as Ps. 119:18, "Open thou mine eyes, that I may behold wondrous things out of thy law."

IV

A fourth foundation stone in the theology of a praying church deals with prayer for others. Our prayer workers are taught this also: *Intercession is not optional! We are to pray for others because Jesus said we should. Scripture is replete with instructions that those who take part in the church that is striving to be God's church will be praying for their fellow members.*

"Who am I to pray every day for someone else?"

"Goodness, I'm not *that* much of a saint!"

"I think it's a great idea, but I don't know *the first thing* about it."

"I have all I can do to manage my own religious life."

These are typical comments of church members who are invited to take part in the creation of a "house of prayer." They are usually sincere first-reaction statements of honest feelings. Most folks come into membership as amateurs in intercession. Have we in the church failed to carry over into our modern day this particular mark of the early household of God?

The book of Acts, in describing the foundings of the Christian movement, is not one chapter old until it tells us that the establishers of the church came

25

together in the Upper Room, and "these all continued with one accord in prayer and supplication" (Acts 1:14). If we hold that this does not specifically tell us that their prayers were intercessory we turn to the apostle Paul. As we read we find him passing on instructions which leave no question that he held this in top priority: "I exhort therefore, that, *first of all,* supplications, prayer, intercessions, and giving of thanks, be made for all men" (I Tim. 2:1). If we attempt to sidestep this directive by suggesting that he was talking to Timothy only, we move to that wise old teacher who summed up the duties of "the twelve tribes scattered abroad" with four plain words—"Pray for one another" (Jas. 5:16).

It will be soon evident to any serious reader of the New Testament that prayer for others was a large part of the work of Christ's church.

In the next chapter we will observe how the prayer life of a congregation reaches out to touch other areas of the church's life and of the individual's complete existence. We say, both to our prospects and to those who have joined, "Certain things are expected of you if you become a part of the Kingdom-building in this place. One of these expectations is that you will study prayer. We ask you to do this that you may grow until you can assume some of the intercessory work of this congregation. Prayer for others is not optional. It is a divine directive from the Lord to his household.''

On page 105 we describe further that pattern of prayer which we teach our prayer workers. We have set out here certain theological concepts which undergird this program and to which we keep coming back in all our training.

The reader will understand that this is not *all* the theology which is taught by our church. Our denomination has a thorougly prepared, Scripture-based statement of belief contained in our Confession of Faith. Such major concepts as the sovereignty of God, sin and salvation, atonement, redemption, election and grace; eternal life and the Lordship of Christ; the kingdom of God and the church as the covenant community; these and others loom large in our teachings. In this chapter we have limited ourselves to a very brief treatment of those theological bases which relate particularly to the creation of a praying church.

Chapter III

Call to Disciplined Living

PRAYER IS NOT THE ONLY WORK OF THE Kingdom. Worship and study, teaching and fellowship, giving and witness, these and many other vital matters need cultivation by dedicated churchmen. Although the full Christian life has only one center it does have many sides.

In Memorial Drive Church we teach our people that prayer is only one of five disciplines calling for Christian dedication. These are brought to the congregation's attention in our "Five Check Points for Growing Members."

A folder which lists and explains these check points is made available to all members for their consideration. It is presented to new members on the day they join. From the pulpit and through our evangelism callers those contemplating membership with us are urged to give serious consideration to these challenges. Bookmarks have been printed and our members are requested to use them in their daily readings. Wallet cards are distributed and we ask our people to carry them in their purses, place them under the glass on their office desks, and generally acquaint themselves with their challenge. They are printed frequently in our parish paper and in the Sunday morning bulletin. Many copies are taken regularly from our literature racks.

The full text of our explanation sheet follows:

FIVE CHECK POINTS FOR GROWING MEMBERS

1. Study diligently   2. Worship regularly
3. Pray daily   4. Give systematically
5. Serve faithfully

What do these mean?

When we joined the church we said "Yes" to this question: "Do you accept Jesus Christ as your personal Saviour and seek to make Him the Lord of your daily life?" But for most of us this was only a starting point. Becoming a mature Christian is a process of growth. It requires effort and devotion and surrender of our will to his will.

So we do not come to our church asking, "What can you do for me?" Rather we come with sleeves rolled up and hearts bent low asking, "Lord, what will you have me to do?"

The greatest fact about religion is summed up in the three words of I John 4:8—"GOD IS LOVE." But this is not a love which allows us to have our own way. It is a love which guides and teaches, directs and calls us to ever higher levels of Christian dedication.

There is a Cross at the center of our faith. It is a mighty symbol of what God has done for us. But when we discover the lost half of the theology of the Cross there comes crashing in on us this truth: THE CROSS IS ALSO A SYMBOL OF WHAT WE MUST DO FOR OUR LORD.

Jesus said, "If any man will come after me, let him deny himself, and take up his cross daily, and follow me." (Luke 9:23.)

The church offers us one sure place to grow in inner relationship to a demanding Lord. Here are five disciplines by which we respond to the love of God. Each member of the church is challenged to constantly check his churchmanship against these revealing questions:

1. *Study Diligently*

Have I taken the "Lessons in Discipleship" taught by the elders and passed the examination at its conclusion?

Do I attend a church school class or participate in one of the church's small groups for Christian growth?

Have I developed a personal spiritual study program on my own?

2. *Worship Regularly*

Do I attend church services every week unless there are providential reasons for not observing Sabbath worship?

Do I pray for the pastor, the choir, the worldwide church as I worship?

Do I extend my hand when the worship is over as a symbol of the love of Christ for all men?

3. *Pray Daily*

Do I participate in family worship in my own home?

Sometime each day do I have a "quiet time" for prayer and listening?

Am I growing in my prayer life toward that day when I can assume some of the tremendous intercessory responsibilities of my church?

4. Give Systematically

Am I a percentage giver and have I studied "Counting the Cost" which states my church's official teaching on this matter?

Do I give my offerings to the church first as a symbol of God's priority on my possessions?

Am I growing in my stewardship as Christ wants me to grow?

5. Serve Faithfully

Am I serving in the church's program or am I preparing for the day when I can assume some position of service in my church?

Am I witnessing to others who do not know my Lord or have no church home?

Am I seeking to serve by living the gospel in my home, community, work?

These disciplines are not standards which indicate that we have arrived. We are not saved by works. We are saved by receiving the unmerited, redeeming love of God in our hearts. But God's covenant of grace is extended to man in such a way that it requires complete and utter faithfulness in the heart which receives him.

This church does not expect perfection from its members. But it does expect growth from sincere surrender to the indwelling Christ.

"As the body is dead when there is no breath left in it,

so faith divorced from deeds is lifeless as a corpse.''
(*James 2:26 NEB.*)

*Are There Evidences in My Life That Christ Is
Having His Way with Me Through His Church?*

When these five check points and the accompany-
ing explanation were first introduced they were en-
titled ''The Pastor's Five Check Points.'' Our
denomination, like all Protestant communions, cher-
ishes freedom of the pulpit. It would have been ac-
ceptable for me to present them at a worship service without previous consideration. In this case,
however, because it was hoped that they would become a serious part of our congregation's life, I
introduced them first to the leaders. The form in
which we now use them is the result of almost a
year's debate and reshaping. No public mention was
made of this until a majority of the officers ap-
proved.

Even then they were ''the pastor's'' because some
of the leaders were strongly opposed, some were
mildly negative, and others wanted to test the feeling before stamping them with their approval.

Following the first pulpit presentation there were
mixed reactions. Some were violent as represented
by a phone call which came on Monday morning. The
lady was very irate and she asked me to count her
out. She said she wanted a church where she could
32

attend on Sunday morning and nothing more. She predicted that we would lose many people and that it was too bad since we had a chance to become the biggest church around "if we would get off this awful demanding kick." She asked if it wasn't all right to have a little fun in life. She wanted to play golf and bridge and do other things besides church work. She didn't want a church that was always needling her about her personal life. Then she concluded that she was going next Sunday to join another church. She wished us good luck but said she thought we were biting the hand that feeds us.

This was indeed a phone call remarkable in its candor. One cannot but tip the hat to honesty in any form. There have been others who reacted like this and more who went away. But it soon becomes clear at the start of any new challenge that there is sure to be opposition. Some of it is pure laziness. Some is the fruit of man's emotional struggle for security in sameness. "Come weal, come woe, my status is quo!" is written indelibly across some minds which want no part of anything new. We followed each of the departers in love and sought their reconsideration in frank discussion.

But there were many more who for the first time began analyzing their churchmanship. Some sought, and are continually seeking, to bring their Christian performance out of the abstract into the definite by these and other self-imposed disciplines. It is our im-

33

pression that these five check points have wrought a good thing in many hearts. We know now from experience that our church has become more vital by spelling out what is expected. By action of the boards of the church these tests have now officially become "The Officer's Five Check Points," and there has been some urging to make them the action of the congregation as a whole.

The positive side of public reaction is stated in the words of one of our current officers who was a marginal member at the time of their first presentation. In witness to a group of new members he testified in these words:

When I first heard these check points for growing members I did a slow burn. No one was going to tell me how to live. But I decided to take a second look. Then I got to reading the book of Acts and I saw that the price of admission to the early church was sacrifice and danger and sometimes death. So I took to thinking that my service club asked better attendance of me than my church. My country club required bigger dues than my church. My business couldn't exist on the kind of performance I was giving my church.

So I put the five check points in my billfold and started to think about them seriously. I'd take them out sometimes and put them on my windshield visor when I drove to work. When I did this it began to come clear why I wasn't getting much out of my church. I wasn't giving much to it. So I began trying to do better and today I just want to tell you that you'll get out what you put in. I'm a long way from what I should be. I know God loves us whether we love him or not. But how much we experience his love is up to us. I want you to know my experience is that the Lord can only do for you in direct ratio to how much you do for him.

Surely the church in modern America should be evangelistic. It should invite people to its services and seek in every way to win the unsaved. But it is simply not so that the whole purpose of the church is to win more members. This *is* a purpose and a great purpose. But the ever-deepening commitment of those who have already been won is also prime work. The church is a missionary movement. But it is also a divine workshop. *Bringing the lost into the fold is only what it should be when those within it are giving their all toward the development of a beloved community worth bringing the lost into.*

Why shouldn't the church say to its prospects, "This is what we expect of you. Are you truly ready to commit your time, your money, your soul?"

It has been our experience that such a declaration has an invigorating effect. It stirs the spirit in those who have already "joined up," and it brings to prospects a solid statement which cautions their hurried decision. Most of the people who place their membership with us have attended for several months before accepting the call to discipleship. Some go for one, two, three years in deliberation before they affiliate. This does not mean that we have

35

no concern for these who are not yet ready to take this step. Our parish program, our officers and pastors, our men, women, and youth minister to many who look to us for spiritual help and call this "their" church in emergencies or in their everyday needs. But by these five check points we have spelled out clearly some norms against which the Christian life can begin taking measurements.

It should be clearly understood that we are not receiving 100 per cent performance from those on our rolls. Adequate provision is made for the weak and the limited. But by every means possible we present the challenge and pray that the Holy Spirit will convict, redirect, and bring into line with God's purposes those hearts which respond. We repeat often the statement that "these disciplines are not standards which indicate that we have arrived." They are starting places where souls center down and lives begin to be changed. They are leavening factors which we hope will go on into eternity until one day they leaven the whole lump.

Since introducing these check points we have found that, from both former members and new, we are getting better performance than we had known formerly. It is easier to staff our church, to raise money, to secure evangelism callers, to bring people into neighborhood study groups, and *there is a much more serious interest in prayer than we have experienced heretofore.*

We conclude that modern Americans like to be challenged to toe the line. They like to be called to deeper dedication. They *want* the church to declare itself and they *will* respond when the call is loud and clear and specific.

I am often asked in ministers' seminars or in visits to local congregations whether there are not grave dangers in this approach. There are, and the critics are right to be concerned. One such feeling of caution is represented by those who ask, "Aren't you afraid you'll create a society of ingrown pietists? Won't some of these folks think of themselves as 'the real church' with others not quite so holy?"

This is a genuine threat and we need to be constantly on the alert for the seeds of self-righteousness.

In my final year at the seminary I thought I knew a great deal. A favorite quip among the students was the old saying, "You can always tell a senior but you can't tell him much!" My professor of practical theology sensed that I was beginning to think I had arrived, so one day he called me to the front of the class. To my side he called the shortest member of our student body. "Shedd," he began, "you are a big man. Physically you are the biggest man around. Now Kennedy here is very small. In fact, he is the smallest man in our school. I hope you both have a good time in Colorado where both of you are going to preach. But one day for your own good, do stand

37

together at the foot of Pike's Peak and notice that compared to the mountain neither of you is very large!''

It was a telling blow to my ego and it drove the point home. We need, in all we do, to be constantly wary of the tendency to self-congratulations. But the surest answer for individual or church is to compare ourselves neither against what we have done nor against what others may be doing but against the true call of Christ to his own. By this standard any church will soon recognize that whatever growth it sees is a distant eternity removed from what it ought to be. The discipline-seeking church will do well to emphasize not only God's love but man's sin and his perpetual need of a strong Saviour.

Other questions frequently put to us by the dubious touch on the prayer programs themselves. These questions take shape as, ''Is this just a group of people praying for their own needs? Do they do anything else besides their prayer work? Are they helping to carry other parts of the church's work?''

These too are well asked. There must be no conflict between the prayer groups, the prayer chains, the prayer workers, and the whole program of the church. Actually, when they are healthy efforts, they are lending strength to the entire body. As the praying members learn to live by the inner communion they charge the entire church with new power. Without the larger context of the church's program such efforts do have a tendency to become pious and self-centered. Women's work, youth fellowship, church school, and other larger groupings of the household of God offer a place where those in prayer undertakings can exercise their newfound spiritual insight. We urge each praying member to participate freely in the life of the body aggregate. When he truly prays he becomes a bit of the purifier in the public reservoir. It is our experience that the more one truly grows in personal spiritual development the more he will want to serve the Lord with gladness in other efforts than his own inner commitment. The praying church will be a working church and the real workers in every phase of endeavor will be the praying members.

We can manufacture service for a brief period. We can whip up enthusiasm for the moment. We can produce concern in limited amounts by telling ourselves that we ought to be concerned. But the life which lasts, the service which counts, and the church which builds on eternal footing—these are an inside job.

The call of Christ is a call to get right at the center and to test all we do by the simple question, "Does this life and this church show evidence of the work of Christ from a committed heart?"

Chapter IV

The Undershepherds

WHEN A NEW CHURCH BEGINS THERE are sure to be many meetings. Some of these are given to details of program and organization. But others are for pure reflection on the basic question, "What is the Holy Spirit trying to say to us? What does our Lord want us to be?"

We were in one of these meditative meetings when a young man rose to witness: "Like we were asked to do at our last session, I've been studying my red-letter-edition New Testament to see what Jesus had to say about his church. There are several things I'd never noticed before. One thing that hits me as being awfully real is his statement, 'My house shall be called a house of prayer.' I've been thinking on this a lot these two weeks and I want to ask you this question that keeps coming to me, I wonder what would happen if every member of our church was prayed for every day by someone?"

His simple question became the seed thought of an

interesting discussion. The general conclusion was that this would be good. If we could develop a work where each participant was daily remembered before the throne of God in prayer, this might be worth serious effort. Since none of us was experienced with such a movement we agreed to pray about this daily during the period before our next meeting.

This was the origin of the "Undershepherds" in our church. We began immediately to consider ways whereby each member might be prayed for daily by some other member.

It was almost no time until the Holy Spirit brought us to the naked truth that (a) on the personal level our own prayer life was shallow and ineffective, and (b) we didn't know point one about teaching others how to pray.

I am quick to confess that this is a sad commentary. There were many fine men and women in this organizing group. Some of them had outstanding records of lay leadership in their previous churches. But with few exceptions they were boldly honest as they admitted that too much of their prior efforts had been in the realm of doing for the Lord rather than in the development of personal communion with him.

I joined them as they humbled themselves before this awesome truth. When it came to that kind of

41

prayer which had something left over to share with others, I too was a neophyte. This was most humiliating. When a minister, a few years out of seminary, must admit to such dearth in his knowledge, this is too bad. So, though I hated to do it, I confessed that we were face to face with the scriptural question, "Can the blind lead the blind?" It was a gracious moment for me when they calmly accepted my admission without panic. Perhaps they had suspected all along that theirs was a minor prophet sadly lacking in some essentials.

When the confessional was done we decided as pastor and people that we would set out down the road together toward a church where every one would be prayed for every day by someone.

We began by designating one night each week as a "School of Prayer" when we would study together some of the great prayers of the Bible. Those in attendance agreed that they would dedicate a definite portion of each day for serious study of prayer. Then we would come together and share our insights and help one another. We would supplement our Scripture searching with books and pamphlets on how to pray, intercession, and personal spiritual development.

When we had gained enough confidence to undertake it we divided the church membership into groups of seven families to each prayer worker.

42

We started with no other goal than that each member of each family would be prayed for daily by name. It was not long until we discovered that, for most of us, this was an impossible number. Those of us who had never disciplined ourselves to daily prayer for others could not do an adequate work with that many people. So we reduced our groups to four and today we find that our best work is being done by those who have no more than two or three families in their care. Some have only one, and we allow each prayer worker to set his own limit up to four.

Today there are more than 250 people in our congregation who are called "Undershepherds." The name might be almost anything else which would serve the purpose. This particular name was chosen because it symbolizes service "under the Good Shepherd." We refer to this meaning on occasion, but usually it carries its own meaning.

When the Holy Spirit sets to work on a group of people it is well to allow plenty of flexibility for new developments. We began with the simple covenant that we would pray daily for every person in our assignment and that was all. But it was not long until some of the Undershepherds wished for regular personal contact with those for whom they prayed. Some determined to call at the home involved. Others decided to ask the people for whom they were praying to pray for them. Still others

43

wished to share with them materials for their own devotional life. Out of this grew our present request that an Undershepherd call each quarter in his assigned homes and that he deliver our denominational devotional guide to his flock. Some wished to invite these families into their own homes either individually or in groups. Almost all who were serious about their prayers requested that we notify the Undershepherd in case of emergency or illness. This resulted in some outstanding cases of members ministering to members in their time of need.

Gradually it became plain that one effect of the Undershepherd program would be that of giving the ministry back to the people. Any student of the book of Acts will quickly observe that this was a strong factor in the early church. They cared for one another's needs to the extent to which these needs were made known.

In other churches where I have served as pastor, the personal needs of the people were made known mostly to me. As a clergyman, I was the principal burden bearer. This was due to several factors. (*a*) It was expected. I was the paid professional who was called by the congregation to do this work. (*b*) The people did not really know one another's needs. Most folks hesitate to share their inner problems without first experiencing an intimate interchange of the externals. Before there can be such sharing there must be the knowledge that these personal af-

44

fairs will meet with loving concern. (*c*) There was no congregational development by which this loving concern might be expressed person to person. It is true that we cannot manufacture the fellowship of love. This is the gift of God. But sometimes it is up to us to provide channels through which the love of God can flow.

Today in the Undershepherds work of our church I find myself being by-passed frequently as members of the flock call their Undershepherd rather than their pastor. On a recent day in one of our hospitals I arrived at a bedside early to be there before the appointed operation. As I entered the room I found my place already occupied by an Undershepherd. The sensitive "sheep," worried lest I take offense, apologized for not calling me and let it go at that. But during her period of recovery she broached the subject again and once more said she was sorry that she had failed to call me. I assured her that nothing could have made me happier than to find one of her own church members taking my place. Whereupon she laughed in relief, and then leveled with me in delightful candor, "I guess the real reason why I called him was that I knew he was praying for me every day, and I wasn't sure you would be!"

Lest there be concern that the pastor might be replaced in an Undershepherding church, I hasten to say that there is still sufficient work to justify a clergyman on the staff. Sometimes Undershepherds

45

call me when they need to verify their handling of intimate personal problems. With these I see myself as the "checking" minister prepared to counsel with the "real" ministers. It is also true that such lay ministry is still not a 100 per cent performance, and my time is well taken up with caring for those who do not or cannot render such ministry. But as the years pass, we find a genuinely growing movement toward the ministry of the laity in our church.

Out of the early start here described and through the leading of the Holy Spirit we have now come to the place where we ask those who undertake the work of an Undershepherd to commit themselves to certain "basic" undertakings. These are summed up in a leaflet which we send to those invited to this work. The text of this brochure follows:

WHAT THE UNDERSHEPHERD DOES

1. *He prays daily for each member of his flock.* This is his first responsibility and he is asked to make a personal covenant between himself and the Lord toward this end.

2. *He delivers the quarterly devotional guide to the home.* In cases where he is out of the city or otherwise indisposed he is asked to (a) mail the guide with a note of explanation or (b) call his subleader who sees that the devotional is delivered.

3. *He ministers to special needs within his group.* When there are known emergencies—death, illness, hospitalization, or other crises—the church will notify the Under-

shepherd. The Undershepherd is asked to do the same for the church when he receives this information first.

4. *He checks attendance of his flock members each Sunday.* He will make an effort after worship to speak to each one in his care. He will contact personally those whose continued absence gives him concern.

5. *He will encourage members of his flock to attend the "Lessons in Discipleship."* Since he himself has passed the examination for this course, he knows the value of this education and strongly recommends it to those for whom he prays.

These are the five "basics" in the Undershepherd's endeavor. Daily prayer will doubtless lead to other activities. We have many Undershepherds who give an annual dinner, tea, or get-together for their people. Some flocks join together for Fourth of July picnics or other festive occasions. There are Bible study groups, bridge clubs, and regular downtown luncheon gatherings of certain Undershepherds and their flocks who have built up a feeling of togetherness in this experience. Husbands and wives often make their calls together. Some of our Undershepherds ask their children to pray for particular children members in their groups. We ask each Undershepherd to follow the lead of the Holy Spirit as he uses his God-given imagination. This is a service of love and the cornerstone is DAILY PRAYER FOR EVERY MEMBER. This will not be easy. But you have learned by now that full following of the Christ who gave his all for us requires discipline, steady practice, and commitment.

We will be calling you in the near future. At that time we will invite you to attend a seminar for further details, plus a question and answer period. You may give us your decision at the conclusion of this session.

Meanwhile will you please be meditating on such scripture selections as these:

John 13 :35	Acts 1 :14
Rom. 12 :10	Gal. 5 :13
I Thess. 3 :12	I Tim. 2 :1
Jas. 5 :16	I John 4 :21

These verses have helped us to know what Christ wants from us. They give us insight into the fellowship of love which was the New Testament church.

We do not ask for perfect performance. We do not expect success all at once. What we need is those who are willing to try the discipline of daily intercession out of loving concern for others. This is what the Undershepherd does—he loves, he cares, and he prays daily for his fellow members.

Thank you for considering this, the most important work in our church.

The reader will note our steady emphasis on the church member's responsibility to concern himself with some other member in prayer, in care for his needs, and in attention to his spiritual welfare through worship and instruction. He will also observe our emphasis on this work not as a man-made program but as a call of Christ to create the New Testament church in modern society.

Through our early studies we became convinced that this was an authentic scriptural development in our particular local situation. The more we studied the more it came clear to us that in the early church, as reported in the book of Acts, (*a*) people loved one another in genuine prayerful concern and (*b*) the priesthood of believers manifested itself in laymen doing the major ministry.

It is a sad fact that in our modern church many local situations rise and fall on the personality of the parish minister. There is nothing wrong with winning friends and influencing people if this is done on the high level of pointing the won toward the Lord. Through these pastors, who have been gifted with winning ways, or who have personally developed this to the maximum, souls have been saved and churches have been strengthened.

But the alert thinker will rightly suspect that this does not bode well for the future. First, some of us are not as naturally gifted as others. Second, this personality-centered Protestantism tends to a dangerous ambivalence over the years. As ministers come and go, local churches move up and down on the yo-yo of "like him"—"don't like him." Third, even if we were one of the darlings of public relations we would surely realize that this is not what the church was meant to be.

It is imperative that we discover some media whereby Christ becomes the focal point of the church's life. In such a church, where people are gathered about him, the church takes on a personality of its own. There is no higher goal for those of

49

us fortunate enough to be parish ministers. To lead in the creation of a congregation where Christ is central; where his people are sharing his love in all the warmth of that experience; where the church is being used by him for redeeming individuals, recreating the community, and winning the world—this is the stuff of prime purpose for all of us in positions of church leadership, clergy and laity alike.

The Undershepherd program in our particular parish sets its sights on such a goal. We have been with this development long enough now to witness that the church moves toward becoming *the Church* when people pray. In the seven years of our Undershepherds at work we have witnessed many miracles of his grace working through his praying people. And on the horizon we see visions of a church with his personality. We look for the day ahead when the ministry of the laity becomes the predominate tone of this church's life. We are a long way from where we hope to be, but it is our testimony that Christ does draw his own to himself, he does work his miracles of love, he does use the church wherever serious disciples pray daily in earnest intercession for the flock.

Chapter V

The Undershepherds at Work

HOW ONE CHURCH INITIATED THE Undershepherd program may be helpful for those considering such a movement. The church is located in a small town in the Southwest. The pastor is a young man who was prayerfully determined to break up some ancient thought patterns heavy on the "do nothing" side. These had been "Sunday folks" for a long time. They let him know quickly that they wanted few activities during the week, and they certainly wanted no part of making calls. They were completely satisfied with nothing but worship. Naturally in this kind of setting they had many inactive members. But the young minister refused to sit "at ease in Zion" as they wanted him to do.

One night at board meeting he took along some 3 x 5 cards with the names, addresses, and phone numbers of certain families who hadn't darkened the door for months. They were still on the rolls, but their long absence indicated complete disinterest.

51

He began the meeting with some verses of scripture about the New Testament church. He read passages on intercessory prayer and the importance of caring for those who had fallen away. Then he told the officers that he intended to take three of these cards and pray every day for each of these families for one month. He told his eight elders that he would appreciate their each taking three and doing the same. He explained that next month they would exchange cards and add some more. He made it clear that this was an experiment and they would see where it might take them.

Only four of the men took three cards each. The next month one dropped out but two others, encouraged by the reports, decided to join forces.

The big break came when a rough old lumber dealer beamed as he reported how two of the people for whom he prayed came to church for the first time in months. Under cross-examination he admitted that he had driven out to the country to call on these folks. But he defended his action vigorously by confessing that nothing but prayer could have moved him to make that call. He told how he had struggled against the urge to go. But at last he went. He said their first response was, "First time anyone from the church has ever been here when they weren't asking for money." But their second response was a return to church.

Much to the young pastor's delight, one elder followed this witness by suggesting that they tell the congregation what they had been doing. He also moved that they invite others in the membership to share this praying for their fellow members. This was the beginning of a vital prayer movement which awakened a dormant congregation and paved the way for real spiritual growth with these people.

Those considering such a program for their church will be interested in other specific statements from particular churches that have adopted the Undershepherd movement here presented. The following are selections from a variety of reports in our files. They represent different denominations, widespread locations, and divergent parish types. The first witness is from a Midwest church of considerable wealth and executive clientele. The second represents an oilfield church of laboring people. The third stems from a typical American county-seat town.

"Something is happening in First Church"—this comment was made by a panel member at the congregational meeting last Wednesday evening. The consensus was that the "something" was very good. Only to look around the room gave ample evidence. That evening occurred on one of the coldest days in the century. . . . Yet, Fellowship Hall was full, and everybody was enthusiastic, cordial, friendly.

The usual "strain" in considering the budget was pleasantly absent. . . .

This time, due to THE UNDERSHEPHERD PROGRAM . . . , the pledges were in, a substantial increase was shown, and the budget . . . voted upon without a murmur.

We looked back on four months of successful Christian experience; then we looked to the future, realizing that there are infinite possibilities in the years ahead with the UNDERSHEPHERD PROGRAM.

(This testimonial is taken from the congregation's weekly newsletter. Four months prior to the meeting cited here, the church began to pray daily for every member. This church was founded in 1872. It has a membership of sixteen hundred.)

Since we established the principle of prayer each day for every member, real miracles of love are taking place. Those who have been here from the beginning tell us there is a new spirit of Christian concern and fellowship never felt before with our people.

(The witness here is a layman who heads the Undershepherd Program in a church of 175 members. It is located in a coastal town. The congregation is eleven years old.)

Shades of the New Testament church. We are experiencing a real rebirth. For the first time our officers are beginning to pull together as a team. Even the choir has quit fussing and started growing. We've had to buy new chairs for church school and for overflow at worship. The daily prayers of the Undershepherds are literally remaking this old church.

(These words come from a pastor in a county-seat town. His church is seventy-four years old. It has 450 members.)

These unsolicited testimonials bear out the fact that great things take place when local churches start a program in prayer. The Undershepherd work of our congregation has come to the attention of others through various media. Books and magazines have published brief statements or written feature articles describing the prayers of our people.

We have been encouraged to study unusual approaches of those who have adapted our program to the lay ministry of their own members. Some interesting innovations have been added in particular congregations.

A Methodist church in North Carolina has divided its parish into Undershepherd units. Each unit consists of twenty families under one Undershepherd. These groups meet monthly with the Undershepherd in a selected home. Sometimes they meet for covered-dish dinners, sometimes for dessert. The opening period is given to visiting and fellowship. Then the Undershepherd or an appointed officer leads in a Bible study or group discussion or some selected assignment. Before the group breaks up for the evening, names are drawn and each family partipating is asked to pray daily for the selected members. The pastor of this church reports a vitally growing sense of oneness within the congregation. Advantages of this approach are obvious. They include study together and loving concern for specific fellow members. Obvious disadvantages are the necessity for follow-up on non-attenders and those who do not care to participate in such meetings. But the minister says, "We feel that we are making a meaningful approach to the New Testament church."

A church of another denomination in the Southwest makes new Undershepherd assignments each month. Each member prior to the first of the month receives a card with the name of a fellow church member for whom he is to pray daily during the month. Names are kept secret unless the member wishes to reveal himself to the person for whom he prays. This pastor wrote that much has been accomplished since this program was begun. New friendships have been formed and "in one case an old enmity is being breached which everybody said could never be healed."

Other variations are applied as the local situation requires. All of them seem to indicate that new life is possible in old patterns where any congregation sets out to truly establish a praying church.

Many congregations have developed other plans for keeping the fellowship intact. Parish plans, zone plans, neighborhood groupings, officer responsibility-assignments, friendship and "buddy" plans are used to keep the church together in manageable units. These are worth much when they work and they are to be praised insofar as they produce the effects of the New Testament church in modern garb.

It is this pastor's personal experience that some of these tend toward the dangerous point of becoming mere ecclesiastical machinery unless they are set squarely on the foundation of spiritual concern. It is our witness that only the integration of daily prayers into the program can produce the kind of Christian care which truly ministers and increases in love as the years pass. But when people are brought into prayer for other people, good things do happen in the local church.

Those considering some variation of this plan will be interested in scenes from the Undershepherds at work in Memorial Drive Church:

The little old lady had a new light in her eye on that particular day. At ninety-one she was our oldest member. When I sat down in my usual chair, she brought me some cookies and set them lovingly on the table. As she placed the milk beside me she said reverently, "My new Undershepherd brought me these cookies this morning. Do you know what I think, Pastor? I think my new Undershepherd must really live with the Lord. I've loved my other Undershepherds too, but this one does something no other person has ever done for me except my ministers. She's been to see me three times already and every time before she goes, we hold hands and she prays that God will keep me well and strong. Do you know what it means for a lonely old lady like me when she comes and prays with me? We talk about the church a bit and she lets me tell her how I feel. I guess she must be the best woman in all the world, don't you?"

That day on the way home I made a special trip to see Rosalie. I wanted to thank her for what she had done for Mrs. Ostrom. "Thank me?" she began. "I should thank you. This praying for my flock has done me so much more good than I could ever do them. And, do you know, this is the first time I have ever prayed outloud with anyone except at mealtime? No, I'm the one who should be saying 'thanks!' " (We do not require nor even urge our Undershepherds to pray with their flock members when they call. We only urge them to follow the Holy Spirit's guidance on this matter.)

It was a very plain potted plant on the nightstand in that hospital room. It was drab now and the purple flowers were almost gone. But the patient was leaving them there for a reason. She explained that the little plant was by her bed when she came out from under the anesthetic. Then she handed me the well-worn card which read, "Be a good sheep and get well quick. Your Undershepherd, Frank."

The hours were long and I could tell he was tired. This was the third night in a row that Carl had been sitting by the bed when I came to the hospital in the early morning to see how Dan had made it through the night. From midnight to daybreak the big man had been relieving Sally so she could get some rest from her husband's bedside. She had a family to care for and, like she said, "I don't see how I'd have made it if it hadn't been for Carl. Someday when things settle down we'd like to be Undershepherds too."

These three partings of the parish curtains are examples of our Undershepherd work at its best.

When our program began, the major part of the Undershepherd effort was carried by the officers of the church. As our congregation grew, this situation changed until most of the Undershepherds now are not serving on our boards. The change came not only because we needed more Undershepherds than our officers could supply, but we soon found that some men who make excellent official leaders are not equipped for the discipline of daily prayer.

We make it plain to those who begin this work that there is no shame connected with discontinuation. We even make it easy for them to resign without embarrassment by checking a postcard and returning it to the church office. This card is sent out prior to each quarterly date.

All flock assignments are changed each year at the first of April. Exceptions are made in the case of those who have special reasons for continuing with particular people or when a new member has been assigned in the preceding quarter. Many of our Undershepherds are men and women who make this their single service contribution to the church. There are, of course, other cases where church officers, teachers, and leaders of various groups wish to take on the added responsibility of caring for a flock.

Undershepherds are nominated to the board by the minister, the Undershepherd co-ordinators, and the evangelism secretary. This "selection committee" considers its nominations prayerfully, and invitations are extended only after approval by the officers. We have now developed to the extent that members who appreciate the care they have received sometimes volunteer for this work. We operate under the ruling that all Undershepherds must have completed the examination which is given at the end of our "Lessons in Discipleship." This requirement assures that those who serve in this work will have adequate knowledge of the church to share with members of their flock.

We have four types of Undershepherds led numerically by our men. As indicated many of these ask their wives and children to assist them. Women Undershepherds are assigned only to the widows, single women, and divorcées. Our High School Undershepherds serve the children of the church whose parents do not belong. At first we asked our women Undershepherds to care for this group. This was not effective. As one of our women said, "My sheep is more like a mountain goat. Most of the time I can't catch her still long enough to call on her, let alone minister to her." We have found that our young people work best here because they see their charges often at school and they have entrée into the homes which adults do not have. Our fourth group consists of couple Undershepherds whom we ask to be praying daily and caring for one other family in the church. Most of these couple Undershepherds are selected from that group in the church who attend regularly but do not seem to "take" to the church's program in education, fellowship, or other activity. The development of these couples has been an interesting experiment, and some fine friendships have been formed as a result.

All Undershepherds are invited to a seminar before they begin their work. These seminars are held on Sunday morning for the men, women, and high schoolers. The couple Undershepherds meet for a relaxed evening of visiting about the program. Most of the new people are brought into the Undershepherds work prior to the April 1 changeover date. Some are added, however, throughout the year as the need arises. No Undershepherd begins work without attending a seminar. During the fall season we hold a series of "briefing" seminars for all Undershepherds to discuss the overall program, hear their witness, receive their suggestions, and answer any questions.

On the first Sunday in April all of our Undershepherds are asked to participate in an "Undershepherds Comissioning Service" during the worship hour. The litany of dedication used here not only makes a lasting impression on the Undershepherd but has a telling effect on our people as they hear these workers unite in a commitment of love for the members of the church.

A review of the advantages and disadvantages of an Undershepherd program may be worthwhile to those who plan such a development.

One of the most favorable aspects is the large number of nonofficer members who are given definite responsibility. Another decided blessing is that officers who go off the boards by rotation can be continued in active service to the church.

There are many side-benefits to the clergy in such a program. Most ministers feel surfeited sometimes with budgets, building programs, speaking engagements, sermon preparation, counseling, and calling. On too many occasions the parish priest sees himself far afield from the spiritual ministry for which he trained and to which he feels called of the Lord. The "loving concern" of the pastor's heart is often nothing more than a beautiful theory murdered by a gang of brutal facts. It is impossible to describe the inner quiet which comes when one knows that a good percentage of the members of his church *are being cared for by their fellow members.*

An amusing added advantage in this program has been the lack of complaints which have come to the pastor's ears. It is true that some are impossible to please so long as they hold hard to their neuroses. But the finest of people are often sensitive, and in the close intermingling of even the best-run churches feelings will be hurt. For several years there was a notable absence of such complaining coming to me in this parish. I was about to congratulate myself on my newfound ability to win friends and influence people, until I awoke to the realization that *the people were doing their fussing to their Undershepherds.*

Disadvantage number one has been the great blocks of time consumed in setting up such a program and keeping it moving effectively. It will be obvious that numerous planning hours are required of the minister and those in charge of this work. We attempt to keep well ahead of the program at all times and continually go over our rolls for future potential workers. But this has a valuable adjunct,

63

namely an ongoing check of our membership for those who are not participating, or for those who are losing interest or drifting away. But such a program does cost dearly in time, thought, effort, and energy. During our early days most of the hours required in setting up such a program were given by volunteer workers. As our church has grown a paid evangelism secretary has been added to serve regularly in the office and to direct many of the organizational details.

Another distinct disadvantage is the glaring failures in nonperformance. Our judgment is that in any given year our Undershepherd work is only 80 to 85 per cent effective. This is the highest level we have been able to reach. Effectiveness is measured by what the Undershepherds say, what the flock members say, and by the return of the quarterly postcards indicating when the calls have been completed. We have developed a method of distributing the Undershepherds packets containing the devotional guides which gives us at a quick glance those who are not making their calls. It is true that members who are neglected by the non-performers feel even more neglected than if we had no such program.

Another potential flaw which must be carefully guarded against is the temptation to use the Undershepherd program as a tool to promote particular projects within the church. Any live-wire operator for an all-church program sees the Undershepherds as a ready-made force to push his particular efforts. But except for picking up the first pledge (we do not use our Undershepherds on the all-church canvass) and a pre-October reminder of Worldwide Communion, we insist that the Undershepherds are *not* for any other purpose than ministry to the membership by daily prayer and loving concern.

This pastor joins the testimony of many who have discovered this sure fact: Whenever a congregation begins at any point to center down in prayer, God engineers new developments which may loosen the constricting lethargy and make possible the deep breathing of the Holy Spirit into the soul of his church.

Chapter VI

The Prayer Chains

"GROUP-THINK" IS A PRODUCTIVE TECHnique for modern business. Brainstorming sessions, when each person offers every thought that comes to his head, make an exciting variation on the progress-is-our-business theme. They say that many fine new products have come from the clatter and chatter of these sessions.

With us, it does not seem to work like this in prayer programs for the local church. In our memory no significant phase of our people's spiritual development has come out of deliberate mental pushing for new ideas. It is true that some startlingly fresh thoughts have originated during group gatherings for prayer. But even these have seemed somehow to come during the least expected times or out of stillness or when the subject was altogether different than we might have planned for launching such a concept.

It has become increasingly clear to us in the development of a praying church that we do not need to clamor at the gates of heaven for fresh insights. God has all the ideas there are, and our responsibility is not so much to be in a mood of inventiveness as to be in a spirit of receptive waiting. Our first need is not to be original but to be open. Where prayer is concerned outward cleverness isn't nearly so important as inner quiet.

This is why it may be wise to approach new prayer undertakings slowly. It is well to come to them with an open mind and ready heart. When one does this, the Holy Spirit may germinate the seed and cause something to grow from it which he knows is best for a particular situation.

Through the years we have shared our effort with ministers and laymen of varied denominations. It has been thrilling to see the way in which specific needs were met for individual churches.

The gentle approach may be in order, especially when thought patterns have become thoroughly set in the history of the local church. Beginning the prayer work in difficult situations calls for unusual perseverance. It might also require careful handling of timid leaders who may be overly wary at the point of "what will people think."

A parish pastor from a small Midwestern town gives eloquent expression to this problem. He describes his predicament in the following excerpt from one of his letters:

My people don't take rapidly to new ideas. Folks here are conservative by nature. Over a five-year period we may not have a half-dozen new families joining us. It seems to me that with the young people leaving our community and no fresh blood coming in, this is the most difficult kind of ministry. I think statistics will show that up to 50 per cent of the churches in our communion are like this. I am convinced that the answer lies in the area of prayer and spiritual development of those folks we do have. But the big question is, How do we start? What is the right way to introduce a deeper spiritual development in a sleepy church like mine?

His blade goes deep and the man is right. It is one thing to launch experimental efforts in a new development. It may be quite another to interest the apathetic or to strike the imagination of those who have long since buried their early enthusiasm.

For those who begin with what looks like a dead-end situation, there are some interesting experiments on record.

A Lutheran pastor from the Great Lakes region said that his officers met him with decided opposition when he first approached them on the Undershepherd plan. They made such comments as: "Never heard of it!" "It would never go here!" and "We're not ready for that."

So he decided to try something else. He quietly went to work lining up people who would agree to

form a "Special Needs" Prayer Chain. They began
with the organist, a young mother, one farmer, the
pastor and his wife.

One Sunday he announced that there were some
people in the church who had agreed to pray for
others whenever they felt the need of someone's
help besides their own. They were disappointed
when not a single request came in two weeks. So he
went to the police chief, the mortician, and the doc-
tors. There were some interesting reactions but no
one laughed and some asked questions.

Then one day the phone rang. It was from the
hospital and would they please pray for this man
who had been in an accident at the mill. They did
and he recovered.

This broke the ice which they thought might
never be broken. Within one year the chain had
grown to eleven members forming a vital Christian
fellowship of concern. They began receiving requests from all over their area. They studied together and have now become a highly respected part
of their church.

It was not long until the matter came again before
the board. One of their most conservative members
witnessed to the personal appreciation of his own
family for what the prayers of the chain had meant
to them in an emergency. The pastor concluded that
other officers expressed a new interest and he wit-

nessed that through this approach they had opened the door to some great things in his congregation.

Our files contain testimonials from other churches in like condition which have started on the road to a praying church through the "special-needs" prayer chain. It is well to note that the Lutheran pastor here quoted *drew up his own plan designed to fit his local needs.* Many people will more enthusiastically undertake something which has been created by themselves or for themselves.

An Episcopal pastor says that he initiated the praying church by asking the women of his Altar Guild to pray daily for certain sick members during Lent. Another launched a similar program at World Day of Prayer services in his church. Still another started this work by soliciting his young people to daily prayer for members of the church who were away at college.

By whatever means, the evidence gathers. It has been our experience that any church which can get any group within its membership praying for others is on its way to a growing prayer life. Word gets around. People talk. Witness comes from unexpected places. Prayer *does* change things, and breakthrough *is* possible when even a few begin to care with the New Testament love which marked the early church. The promise still holds: "Call unto me, and I will answer thee, and shew thee great and mighty things." (Jer. 33:3.)

Our own *Special-Needs Prayer Chain* started one morning at 2:30 A.M. It was during our church's first year of organization. This was Bill Bush calling. He was a member of our Men's Prayer Study Group which met before services on Sunday. They were, at this particular period, studying and praying together on the business of being better fathers. Bill was calling from the hospital, and he said he was phoning members of our group to request their prayers for a premature baby. The newborn son was several weeks early and the doctor said that only a miracle could save this life. So each member phoned another member and in the middle of the night we prayed. And in the morning we phoned others who loved the lovable Bill. They phoned their friends whom they knew would understand. The baby lived.

For seven years the members of our Special-Needs Prayer Chain have been carrying emergency matters to the throne of God for countless people. Any monthly check of our records might find calls from dozens of our own families and from places in faraway states where word of this group has made its way.

Today there are twenty-one men and women in our congregation who are banded together in this special prayer work. By a method which they have developed through the years, in a very few moments any emergency need can be channeled to each person in the group. Members of the chain have covenanted

71

with the Lord to give top priority to their intercessory prayers for a special period. They have prayed
for hospitalizations and coming operations. They
have interceded in behalf of people at court, people
at sea, people in space, people in quandary. They
have prayed for family emergencies, family deci-
sions, family quarrels. Their calls for help number
in the hundreds and vary from general requests to
matters of greatest intimacy. Now and then someone
calls to solicit the special-needs chain for prayers of
rejoicing that guidance has come or emergencies
have met with victory.

It should be clearly understood that this is no
magic circle of wonder workers. Always the emphasis is on God's love and the subject's proper response. It is true that we have had numberless reports of exciting results from such prayer. Healings
and seemingly impossible miracles have followed.
But full healing is more than earthly healing, and
miracles are not always apparent to human eyes.
Our group believes that effective praying is a much
deeper reality than most of us can grasp. Our chain's
efforts are simply to relate the object to the love of
the Lord and leave it in his hands.

A typical prayer of any one of the prayer chain
members is in the order of:

God of all things in their right order, God of blessing and
healing and eternal salvation, here is _____ for

heaven's pure love this day. We would hold him (her) up to your care and pray that he (she) might respond in the right way to the Everlasting Love which is all about him (her). Thank you for your love and for hearing our prayers. Amen.

Simple? Yes! But from this platform of prayer concern the chain member adds those prayers which are within his or her own understanding. Yet the emphasis is always on simplicity and God's love and a full response.

An exact reporting of certain things which have resulted from such praying would make most unbelievable reading. There are breathtaking records within this experience. But we do not publish these and we talk little about them to others outside the group. Such testimonials have a way of being misinterpreted and seeming like false manipulations of the will of God. We also believe that in the wisdom of the Heavenly Father some things which seemed like failures to us may have been miracles in his Kingdom. We do not even understand fully how it happens that finite men can have so much effect for good in relating other lives to the Kingdom. We can only testify that, as the scripture says, "This is the confidence that we have in him, that, if we ask any thing according to his will, he heareth us." (I John 5:14.)

It is obvious that such a group at prayer must be very much in earnest. Our group is continually studying materials on intercession. They meet together quarterly to discuss their activities and dig deep into what they are doing. Each of these meetings is one of the highlights of our church year.

Such a chain as this constitutes a tremendous adjunct to the pastoral ministry. Many times I have actually seen the quieting influence of the Holy Spirit come over some struggling soul when I was able to say, "I will ask my Special-Needs Prayer Chain to begin praying for you today."

We have many witnesses who join with this testimony from a recent letter:

I think the main thing that brought me through my heart surgery was your prayer chain. You've no idea what it meant to me when I was alone on my bed to know that twenty-one perfect strangers were praying in my behalf. I don't think I'd ever have found the courage to make it through without them.

As we said at the outset, once a prayer development of one sort is underway, all kinds of variations are inevitable. The important thing seems to be to start somewhere and let the Holy Spirit do with it as he wills.

The work of our special-needs chain is easily the most exciting phase of our church at prayer. But from this group's work have come several other "chains" made up of people doing specific types of intercession for particular needs.

The Evangelism Chain was our next natural outgrowth of "stirring up the spirit" for prayer. This is a group of people who have covenanted with God to pray for church prospects. It came into being when certain sensitive members suggested that praying only for those who had united with the church was not enough. They asked, "Why shouldn't we have a prayer concern for those in our community not yet affiliated with any church?"

When a family attends our church for the first time they will be visited soon after their initial appearance. If they attend again, their second visit is followed by assignment to the Evangelism Prayer Chain. The chain member begins daily prayer for this new family and continues in prayer according to an agreed-upon plan. This chain meets with the Special-Needs Prayer Chain at the quarterly prayer chain dinner. Here they discuss their work and witness to their most effective methods.

This group does not pray that these particular prospects may become members of our church. Their prayers are rather that these people will be led to a vital relationship to Christ in the church of *his* choice.

One man, who united with the church, when he heard that someone had been praying for him prior to his joining, said: "When I thought about someone who didn't even know me praying for me and my family every day, I got the feeling that I had to

75

know more about what makes people do things like that.'' This man is now one of our most effective Undershepherds.

In the case of each of our prayer chains, their instruction and suggestion sheets are kept on the church literature racks. In this way visitors and prospective chain members have readily available information describing in detail this phase of our church's life.

The Missions Prayer Chain is the largest group participating in our prayer program. It is made up of high school young people. Through the Holy Spirit's leading this unit came into being as a direct outgrowth of the Special-Needs Prayer Chain's influence on one of its own members.

At a meeting of our young people, a young redheaded athlete asked for the floor, and began his speech:

My mom is one of these people who pray for folks when they get messed up. You should see how she's improved since she started this. We ought to have something like this for us kids. Did you hear the missionary last Sunday? He was great. I got to thinking maybe we could pray for people like him.

We studied his proposal carefully and decided to write our Board of World Missions for help in this effort. They responded with enthusiasm and for six years they have been sending us specially prepared sheets with pictures, describing the work of particular missionaries. Prior to the first of each month the sheet on the "Missionary of the Month" is mailed to each of the seventy high schoolers on this chain. The list is divided into four groups with each group assigned to pray for the missionary during one week of the month.

Notice is sent to the missionary from the pastor well in advance of the scheduled month. The missionary is invited to submit special prayer requests from his field. Most of the missionaries respond with enthusiasm. When a missionary's letter is received in time, it is printed at our office and sent along with the monthly assignment. Some of the young people become so interested that they write direct to the missionaries. It is always an interesting event when some excited youngster reads his personal letter from the missionary to the high school class or at the evening youth meeting.

It will be readily apparent that in addition to the good accomplished by the intercession of these young people, we have here a means of (*a*) getting the young to think of needs other than their own, (*b*) personal spiritual development of youth through regular prayer, and (*c*) teaching the mission work of the church to coming generations whose responsibility is to the future of the world.

77

The Pastor's Family at Prayer is another natural outgrowth of a praying church. One year when our church was much smaller than it is now, we decided at the manse that we would pray daily during our vacation for specific families in the church. We wrote a letter to the members telling them that on a certain date in August we would be praying for them. We suggested that on that day they might like to pray for us. We asked them to let us know if there were special needs in their lives for which they wanted us to pray. Our evangelism secretary made up a special notebook listing the names of every family by the dates assigned for their special prayers.

The results of this announcement amazed us. We were literally flooded with prayer requests. They phoned before we left and gave us suggestions for our prayers. They wrote us while we were gone and described special problems on their hearts. And on our return to the parish, person after person told us that on "their" particular day some crisis was met, some problem made clear, some load lifted. Our conclusion is that every family must have something they consider a special need almost daily.

We do not claim to have any unusual knowledge of intercessory prayer by which these people were helped. We feel more often than not like mere neophytes in our understanding of the power of prayer. But we have been led to the inescapable conclusion that the Lord does work in a definite way through

78

the minister's family in their intercession for the parish people.

Since our church has grown beyond the capacity of one month's assignment in prayer, we have altered our original schedule. Currently we are taking two families each day throughout the year. At the first of each month our secretary notifies the church members whose names will be remembered that month. This letter states the dates and again requests their prayers and asks them to inform us of their special requests. The results are the same. Phone calls, letters, personal visits indicate that people do respond to this prayer attention when it meets their heartfelt needs.

Through these prayers we have been led at times to call on particular people whom we have not seen for some time or whom we feel need personal attention. When time permits we phone the families of the day and talk with them about the special needs of their life at this particular time. It is hardly necessary to enlarge on this truth: With many others of our praying members we can say, this kind of praying has done much more for us than it could possibly have done for the families in our prayers.

Chapter VII

Youth at Prayer

THE HIGH SCHOOLERS OF THE CHURCH were holding their fall retreat at an ideal campsite and the moon was high. This was an annual affair with good food, bull sessions, planned recreation, and workshops for the year's program. It was a time to get away for a weekend of serious planning.

We have forgotten most of the details, but we will long remember one incident at the meeting of the committee to plan for social activities. Suddenly Bob threw down his pencil and made a speech. "This masquerade party stuff," he began, "is for the birds. I get fed up with parties."

All ears were tuned. This was not one of the pompous sounding off. Here was the captain of the forthcoming basketball champs. He continued:

How about something different this year? Like maybe one of those prayer groups we've been hearing about? When I hear the preacher say, "Let us pray," I get this funny feeling inside. It's sort of like some part of me wants to get going but doesn't know how. Couldn't we do something about that?

This was the launching of our first youth prayer group. It was a thrilling experience for everyone, including the fortunate pastor and his wife who met with them weekly for five years at the appointed hour. There were lovely girls who grew more radiant through the development of their God-given beauty. There were others whose unwholesome attitudes were redirected. There were national champion swimmers, track stars, and heavyweight wrestlers. There were timid boys with thick glasses and bad complexion. There were straight A students who took the big scholarships and struggling youngsters who floundered in "the sea of D." There were good and not-so-good of both gender. There were negative, positive, sad, happy, popular, rejected, and today the same kind come, longing to respond to God's call and wanting to know how.

Our conclusion is that *young people love to pray*.

The current groups at Memorial Drive Church meet at 6 A.M. They voted for this hour since most fathers in our parish must have the car by seven fifteen to get to their downtown offices. These are city youth. They live in an area where there is considerable distance between members' homes. They attend schools with high-level education that demand serious attention to their studies. They are busy with the teenage whirl. But they come to pray weekly on a chosen date at an unlikely hour because they want to know more about God and how to make contact with him.

We have found this early morning hour best for several reasons. For one thing, participants are fresh. At any meeting there will be varying degrees of attention but in most cases the first thoughts of the morning are sharp because the mind is rested and ready to be filled. Another argument for the early hour is that there are no interruptions and few conflicting engagements. But perhaps the strongest appeal is to the adventuresome spirit of youth. Young folks like to conform in some areas, but they have a definite desire to be different at other points. They seem to possess a subconscious feeling of sacrifice to make the meeting at an hour when the rest of the world is asleep.

"How Do We Start?" is an initial question of those who are interested in this facet of the praying church. In fifteen years' experience with youth at prayer we have found the most effective launching pad to be two or three key young people who have a vital interest in personal spiritual development. Those initiating the promotion among the youth themselves must have ready acceptance by the majority.

Some of our groups have commenced with four. We have had as many as thirty regulars. This is too many. Eight to twelve is the ideal number, and two or three small groups will be more effective than one large unit.

When several have been interested they are called together to discuss plans and pray for guidance. The opening date is announced and for at least the first few sessions we ask a phoning committee to call the prospects the night before the meeting. Generally we follow the pattern of our other prayer study groups described in the following chapter. But we vary the program considerably since young people enjoy experimentation and take readily to innovations.

Contrary to popular opinion, young people do like discipline if it is of an agreed-upon nature and something which helps them grow spiritually. Each group will have plenty to say about its own promises to the Lord. But the key here is simplicity. For youth at prayer, two or three disciplines kept are worth a longer list which tends to become vague and burdensome. Patience is imperative. It will take the average group of young people some time to "groove-in" to disciplined living. Some will be with it for a time and then fall away from the disciplines while they continue to attend. We do not ask for a show of hands of those who are really "with" the disciplines. Some will think one thing is meant, some another.

83

Some have been diligent in the past, but have slipped that week. Some have never missed a day and have an embarrassing way of showing it. Our rule is to mention the disciplines at least once each month, bear down hard on their importance, but let each individual work it out in his own way as God directs.

Drop-ins and drop-outs are frequent with youth at prayer. Some come out of curiosity. Others will remain as permanent members. Drop-outs may run as high as 50 per cent from the beginning of a given period to its end. This is to be expected with young people. There are several reasons for decline in interests. The disciplines may be too much. The material may not be interesting for certain minds. Something different may have been expected. New influences for good and bad could have entered this life. Possibly they have become involved with other activities which usurp their schedules and their energies. There may be personality conflicts. Only God knows some reasons and perhaps the absentees themselves couldn't explain. Some of these will have been helped, even by a brief attendance. Some are not yet ready, and some may have been honestly led by the Lord to step aside. We try to be sensitive to the needs of each member; we express concern at a first absence or a second, but we do not badger nor harass. God works differently in different lives and in ways which he knows best. A few, going all the

84

way, will make this the most important business of some young hearts and that knowledge is enough.

Leadership can make the group, or break it. Whenever possible we select some adult member of the church to assist in the guidance of our youth at prayer. Certain character traits are important for work with the young. *Joy* is one of these. Young people will make their own comedy and their sense of humor comes presharpened. But they respond best to the adult with a happy heart. *Calm* is another must. Most young people are excitable enough without adding a nervous adult to their circle. The effective leader of youth is not easily ruffled. A certain measure of *elasticity* is also important in the "grown-ups" who work with youth at prayer. The ultradignified have their place, but the leader of modern youngsters does well to have in his makeup the gentle stretch of a godly imagination. He should not be afraid to launch out into the unknown. He keeps himself beamed to Divine Insight for the fresh and interesting. He has patience with the unruly, understanding of the odd, and a general "you-can't-knock-me-down" demeanor.

The wise adult leader will remove himself from a prominent position as soon as possible. He may be "in the chair" at the outset but he quickly turns direction of the weekly meeting over to the young people themselves. We have always been surprised

85

at how soon the participants ask to take over. "When can I have a turn?" "Do you need someone for next meeting?" are common questions and frequently come from surprising sources.

At the outset the adult in charge does well to prepare himself with icebreakers. These are questions and thought-provoking ideas which, introduced at strategic moments, pick the group up and get it started again on meaningful discussion. But very soon the "live" group is apt to experience too much rather than too little participation. The adult in attendance will also be alert to draw out those of the group who may be hesitant. He may need a private conference with the youth who tends to overdominate. We ask our adult leaders to meet with the leader for the next meeting or the leader for the month, when such a meeting seems required to make the group effective.

As with our adult groups, we are careful to coerce no one in vocal prayer during the period when the groups pray around the circle. Some very effective members have never been able to pray in any other way than by themselves. Real harm might result when hesitant hearts are overurged. Most young people in prayer groups do not wait long until they begin to pray audibly. At first it may be a mere whisper or a halting sentence but the problem with such groups is likely to soon become a question of setting limits. When the youth prayer group has
86

passed its first awkward stumbling, leaders will find that asking the young to pray is like opening floodgates when souls express themselves before others and the Lord.

The study method varies somewhat from adult groups. Our youth at prayer open with silence. This is usually by candlelight but sometimes assignments are placed at each place by the leader for the day. These may be written on a blackboard for all to see as they enter. After the opening by the leader, prayers may be said by the group. Or the circle of prayer may come at the end of the hour.

The book for study by this group might be some plainly written discussion of prayer. Or it can be some passage from the Bible which the group has selected for daily study. One method which we have found very effective is a system of markings used by the young people in their personal daily study. This approach features three signals which are explained by our instruction slips at one of the early meetings:

Candle—This stands for a new idea. Put a candle by those places where you found a fresh new idea to your thinking.

Arrow—This means you discovered one of your faults in your reading. Put an arrow wherever the author touches one of your weaknesses.

87

Question Mark—This means here is something you don't understand. Ask about it. Maybe someone else will have a candle there or an arrow.

These simple indicators have been a real assistance in our prayer study groups for the young and also at times for adults. They make a natural way to begin the interchange of ideas and create an enthusiasm all their own. They also lend real insight into individual progress and point the way to better understanding within the group.

The most effective schedule for our youth groups has been regular weekly meetings during the school year. It is our experience that given the choice on whether to meet during the summer the groups will always vote to meet the year round; however, having tried this approach at various times, we conclude that a recess is valuable. It tends to make consideration more serious when the meetings are limited to the school months. We also find it best not to meet during exam weeks and at holiday seasons.

Our Youth at Prayer are invariably leaders in other phases of the church's life. They sing in the choir, make up a vital part of the evening youth groups, attend church school faithfully, go to camps and conferences, and serve in various capacities in the overall program of the congregation. As previously stated, our youth Undershepherds are selected from these young people with prayer experience. In addition, most of them take places of leadership in school activities and in community affairs. Youth at prayer seem to hear the call of God to testify in their own effective way at opportune times, and by dedicated lives they become a leavening factor wherever they go.

The Fellowship of the Cross is one of the most telling witness movements of our church young people. It is an added discipline for the spiritual life developed by those who wish some way to discuss religion in a natural manner. The members of the Fellowship of the Cross are given a small block of redwood. It is five-eighths inch square, unfinished but waxed. A screw-eye, dipped in glue, has been fastened into the block in order that it may be worn on a necklace, bracelet, key chain, or attached to a notebook. Some hang it in their car or otherwise display it where their friends will see it.

Those who wear the block make three promises: First, "I will pray and read my Bible every day." Second, "I will love my church, work in it, and try to win another person to it or to The Fellowship of the Cross." Third, "I will live every hour with the presence of Christ by my side."

But a fourth big promise remains. Wearers of the block have agreed that when someone approaches them in the hall, at the party, on the street, or any-

89

where to say, "Why do you wear that?" they will answer, "If you have time I'll tell you." They explain the disciplines and ask, "Would you like to wear one? We don't limit this to our church nor to our school. If you would like to make these promises, think it over for forty-eight hours. If you still want to wear it, I'll give you this block and get another for myself."

There are various ways by which the blocks may be distributed. We have found it most effective to make the presentation at our Sunday evening youth fellowship meetings. We limit this to our high school and junior high young people. Immediately prior to adjournment, The Fellowship of the Cross disciplines are explained briefly and the leader announces, "If there is someone who has given his block away, or if there is some person here who has never worn one, you may make your commitment tonight. We will all bow our heads and if you want one, hold out your hand palm up as an indication that you are ready to make these promises. If you need more than one block, hold out your other hand with the number of fingers showing how many you need."

During the period of silent prayer the leader then passes through the group, dropping a block in each outstretched hand. He closes with a word of prayer, asking God's guidance in this witness.

This added discipline was introduced to our youth work because many young people like to talk about religion but they need a natural way to do this. Several thousand of these blocks have been distributed in the schools of our city. They have now made their way into other areas as well and are being worn by young people of every Protestant denomination and by their Roman Catholic friends as well.

The making of these blocks provides an occasional "workshop" for the Sunday evening fellowship meetings. Those who initiate it will find that it first takes a school by storm and is even aborted to odd ends. But those who stay with it will see it gradually settle down into a quiet way of witness for youth who love to talk about their Lord and about his claims on their lives.

The lasting power of prayer on young lives is attested by the witness of a young husband who was won to a deeper spiritual commitment of his own life by his wife's experience in one of our youth prayer groups. Her vital relationship to the Lord had a lasting effect which, like these things do, touched another heart several years after she left the group.

With their different backgrounds there was a wide gap between them. They had many things in common, but there were also some serious conflicts. Once she gave up and went home. But even when they "settled" this particular quarrel there was still a high wall between them. Sometimes they won-

91

dered if they would ever have a closer relationship.

What did it most, Ned said, was the way Carolyn prayed. It wasn't *what* she did so much as the *way* she did it. She would sit there during her "quiet time" reading her books, thinking about her Bible verses, and then she would be very still.

He was so proud of her for the way she stood up to all their friends at the officer's club in Germany. They called her "country" but they loved her. It was as if the whole group had some place to lean because she wasn't afraid to be different. He liked their response and he loved her for it.

Then tragedy struck their home. They lost their first baby. It was then, he said, she seemed to have some hidden props which he simply had to find. He had been around and seen a lot. But he had never seen anything like she was then. He told her he would do anything if he could be like she was on the inside. She didn't get dramatic. She just said that if he really meant it, she would teach him to pray as she had been taught.

So that is what she did. At first he felt lost, but she told him she knew how he felt. "In fact," she said, "you have to feel lost before you can find the way home in this." So slowly and with the help of her Inner Light she showed him the path to God in his own heart.

On the day after he joined the church, Ned contacted us to express his thanks and share the blessing which had come to them through the power of prayer, shared in a marriage dedicated to living with a Living Lord.

We have had many other phone calls, personal visits, letters, and notes from youth who, some years after, were still feeling the impact of young people learning to pray in a praying church.

Chapter VIII

Growing in Prayer

IN 1954 THE WORLD COUNCIL OF Churches, meeting at Evanston, Illinois, to consider the welfare of "the church," made this report: "It is urgent that the Church come to life in small neighborhoods, . . . where neighbors, church and non-church, gather to think and pray."

One of the hopeful signs in the Christian church today is the increasing number of people who are moving into the zone of God's call through these small groups. There are several of these meeting regularly in our congregation and a typical meeting is described here:

The room is dark. Light from a single candle on the table creates an atmosphere of genuine quiet. One by one, members of the group take their places about the table. They pray. For ten minutes there is no sound save an occasional passing auto—or the phone rings in a room far away—or someone laughs from a front porch down the block—or a dog barks.

No one speaks. All heads are bowed. Each member of the fellowship is centering down in the truth of the promise, "Where two or three are gathered together in my name, there am I in the midst of them."

Then, when he feels the time is right, the leader begins the Lord's Prayer. All join together now in audible expression until the room literally seems to come alive with praise as they end together, "Thine is the kingdom, and the power, and the glory, for ever. Amen."

After a moment's pause, the leader says, "Now we will join hands around the table and pray for those with special needs. Are there any requests?" Gradually they come. A woman tells of her neighbor who faces an operation tomorrow. A man confesses that he is worried about a difficult decision which confronts him this week. Another asks special prayers for some program of the church in which he is involved. The suggestions vary from intimate personal matters to prayers for the coming election of public officials. Then the group prays. The leader has asked that they begin on his right and continue around the circle. He has also stated that whoever does not feel like praying may squeeze the hand he holds indicating that he wishes to pass.

The prayers vary from halting first-time petitions to experts in the art of public prayer. Some are set in the intimate terms of "you," "yours," and the

95

ordinary language of simple conversation. Others use the familiar "thou, thee, thine!" Some use both. They pray for those requests which have touched them particularly. They pray for personal matters which reveal the hidden thoughts of the praying mind. When the circle has been complete the leader prays. He seeks to summarize the feelings of all and remembers before God the requests which have been unmentioned. There is silence again for a few moments and the light goes on.

This is the start of a typical prayer study group meeting at Memorial Drive Church.

Numerous other ways make good beginnings and there are infinite varieties of approach worth trying. Sometimes the lights are left on and the group commences with silent study of a scripture passage written on the blackboard. Or a great religious masterpiece may be the common gathering place for spiritual thoughts. Or a meditational passage from one of the Masters of prayer may be placed at each place for the group's consideration. Any good beginning, tested for a time or initiated by some inventive leader, can serve well. We try to guard against becoming stereotyped and to allow plenty of room for new attempts.

Some excellent books on prayer study groups are available in the bookstores. They offer detailed advice to those interested. We have found them helpful and are grateful for their assistance. It is also true, however, that the best learning here is by experience.

Through the eight years of our work with prayer study groups we have come on "Twelve Musts for Effective Prayer Study Groups at Memorial Drive Church." We offer them here as a simple statement of what works best for us.

1. Regular meeting time
2. Periods for silent prayer
3. Periods for audible prayer following special requests
4. A common study book
5. No pressure on anyone to pray aloud
6. Discussion
7. One-hour time limit
8. Agreed-upon disciplines
9. Daily prayer for others in the group
10. A project
11. A definite period of weeks or months
12. Frequent "blanket" invitations to the entire congregation

One of our most successful endeavors is called "The Daily Disciples." This group meets from October through May. The meeting hour is 9:00 P.M. on alternate Sundays. Adjournment comes promptly at 10 o'clock. Although the time is late it has proved itself good for several reasons. Mothers of small children have seen their little ones to bed; men are beginning to feel a need as they face the responsibilities of the week ahead; evening services are over; the world is beginning to quiet down for the night; there is a sense of "sacrifice" connected with coming late which brings out the concerned and creates by itself a oneness of "caring."

This is a disciplined group which has agreed to set aside one half hour each day for prayer and meditative study. Soon after their first meeting they select a book for their common study. Sometimes the choice proves generally helpful to most of those participating. On other occasions, when the book does not get through to a majority, the selection committee is asked to choose another. Scripture supplements are selected for those books which need additional biblical references.

Projects of these small units will vary by committee selection at the first of each year. We have found it imperative that each group do something specific for others as a reminder that prayer is not a cozy little exclusiveness. Without this the group may grow puffy and ill shaped.

One of the most interesting projects has been daily prayer for public officials. The mayor, the sheriff, legislators, and various political leaders have been included. Letters are sent to these men and a large majority of them respond with genuine appreciation. One national congressman, as an expression of his gratitude for "The Daily Disciples" prayers, sent the church a flag which had flown over the nation's capitol.

Other prayer study groups in the church are made up of women alone. They gather in "The Upper Room" during morning hours. We have had similar groups for men, for young parents, for business women, and, as explained in the preceding chapter, some of our most lasting efforts in this direction have been with our young people.

In the starting of new groups we have found it wise to limit their first meetings to a definite time. We announce that we are organizing a new group which will meet for eight weeks. We make it plain that this will be an experimental group and the participants are asked to come only for the eight-weeks period. Some people will respond more readily to a time-limited group since it seems to offer a natural out if they do not find it to their needs. If there are those who care to continue at the end of the eight weeks period they are brought together into a continuing development.

Each group adopts its own disciplines, its own study book, and its own project. The "yokefellow" disciplines featured in the writings of Elton Trueblood make an excellent suggestion of disciplines for beginners. We have found it helpful for the minister or an experienced prayer worker to chair the opening meetings of each group. But we have learned that, as soon as possible, it is wise to pass the leadership around within the group from meeting to meeting.

Often throughout the year, open invitation is extended to anyone interested. This is imperative because there is no sure way of knowing who in the congregation might be moving in the direction of deeper spiritual commitment. No pressure tactics are used and there is some "coming and going" within each group. Some groups break up after a time if there seems to be a lack of togetherness. Those in charge of the church's prayer program need not be discouraged when this happens. Others will gradually center down into a growing unit where genuine spiritual progress is reshaping lives and the Kingdom is established.

Other study groups of an entirely different nature add much to the spiritual life of the congregation. Memorial Drive Church began in a schoolhouse. For nearly five years it had no building of its own. For this reason it seemed good to gather the members into small units for study of the Scripture. We have regular Bible study groups which meet the year round for fellowship and the searching of God's Word. Some of these have been excellent educational grounds for developing church school teachers. Still other groups meet for study in special interests. One such is our "Christian and Government" group. It gathers together those who are particularly inter-

71280

ested in the application of Christly principles in local, national, and international affairs. Another unit is called "The Alcoholism Study Group." This attracts those of our church, and others in the parish, who need to know more about this growing social problem on the American scene. The scope of such units is almost limitless and varies in theme from such general subjects as "An Overall Look at the Whole Bible" to intimate matters like "Sex Education in the Home." Wherever we find enough people searching in one field we send out a feeler and if there is sufficient interest we gather the group and launch another study unit of the church. It has been our policy to appoint at least one officer of the church to each group for counsel and guidance.

The study-group work which reaches most members in our congregation is known as the "house-church" gatherings. Twice each year for eight weeks we make a concerted effort to bring as many of our people as we can interest into neighborhood study groups. These meet in homes for eight consecutive weeks in the spring and again during the fall months. Elected officials of the congregation are appointed to preside over these gatherings. They follow a specified format and use a study book selected by the leaders well in advance of each set of meetings. Invitation is extended to the entire congregation before each series and those expressing interest are contacted personally by the group leaders. On the eighth

101

night in each series the group is served the Lord's Supper in the home by a guest minister who has been arranged for previously. These particular nights, emulating the New Testament church communing together, are sacramental highlights of the church year for many of our people.

Leaders of those groups that seem to have developed oneness are asked to bring their people together monthly during the intervening period between series. This approach has been a most fertile field for developing Bible study groups, for enlisting church school teachers, and for adding workers to our various prayer developments.

The School of Prayer is an annual feature of our church program which is designed to aid those interested in personal spiritual development. These meetings are open to the entire congregation. Each year finds some attenders who are ''looking it over'' to see if they might have what it takes to serve the church in its various prayer efforts. Again no pressure is used to solicit large numbers.

The School of Prayer varies in format. Sometimes it brings in nationally known leaders in the field who vary their presentations from workshop to lecture to question and answer periods. There is neither required attendance of Undershepherds (except at the first seminar before they begin work), nor of prayer chain members, nor of prayer group participants.

102

Some prefer to work on their own. For these, all discussion of prayer might seem like a babble of voices contributing nothing but confusion to personal progress. Others will attend every session with fervor. With this understanding, we offer regularly the best prayer-education available in various forms but leave it to individual workers to determine their own needs.

Additional training helps are offered through the sermons from the pulpit and by making available prayer materials at the literature racks. A special sermon series on the Lord's Prayer, great prayers of the Old Testament, what Paul said about Prayer, or the Prayers of Christ can be a valuable adjunct to prayer education through regular worship. On Sundays when the sermon has been directed to the prayer theme we often find people gathering at the prayer literature rack for the varied selections offered there.

One of the happy surprises of those who set foot on the path of prayer is the tremendous library of materials available in this field. Hundreds of pamphlets are to be had from various denominational headquarters of most churches. In addition, there are many interdenominational sources providing a wide selection.

"Of the making of books there is no end" and volumes on prayer are no exception. The church li-

103

brary in a praying church can provide another vital arm of prayer training within the congregation. We have found it well to assign responsibility for selection of pieces and books to some discerning persons of good judgment. Not all literature on prayer is adaptable to particular approaches. Some writings are much too involved, some may repel rather than attract the interested, and some may be of a nature in conflict with denominational emphases.

Other phases of the church's life will give added opportunities for education in prayer. As previously stated, we ask our prayer workers to carry service responsibilities in the life of the church. We have learned that God accepts us better on our knees if we have been up and doing when he calls. Since those who pray are prepared to share in other areas, these other areas are more willing to cooperate when we ask them to allow for prayer training in their plans. One such highly successful merger of interests has been our annual College of Family Worship in the adult church school. This exciting series features such themes as "Mealtime Is God's Time Too," "How Good Are Your Family Devotions?" "Dust Off the Family Bible," and "Is There Really a Church in Your House?"

In training for prayer it seems good, again and again, to repeat the fact that no one has the final answer and each person must be given plenty of room to work out his own approach. Whenever we think we have nearly arrived we are likely to meet someone who will convince us that we have been bumping our heads against a very low ceiling.

We keep continually before our workers in prayer the simple five-point outline of the masters. Though it may vary somewhat with various teachers, most of the authorities agree that a total prayer life will find time for: *adoring, confessing, thanking, asking, dedicating.*

This is not the place for a detailed analysis of each of these facets of prayer. Many excellent writings treat these matters at length. We often discuss them in groups and ask our participants to use them as a general outline. But we emphasize the truth that "there are twelve gates to the holy city and a thousand different approaches to effective prayer." It may be of interest to set down a typical talk to new people coming into intercessory responsibilities.

One of our two rules for workers here is "Pray in your own way." You will be interested in how various members do their praying.

Some of our workers say that they do most of their praying in their cars. One day I was riding with one of our prayer chain members. On the sun visor above his steering wheel I noticed a paper fastened with a rubber band. Here he had written the names of those whom he was remembering in prayer. This is not at all unusual. Maybe you will join with those who make a chapel of their automobiles.

A football coach testifies that he does his praying during his morning shower. An executive in a fence company has his secretary list "Undershepherd" on the calendar of his daily duties. He says that if he hasn't remembered his flock by five o'clock, he goes out in the fence yard and does his praying before he goes home to the family.

A lady milliner witnesses: "All day long I meet people. They take lots of time trying on hats. In the interims I pray. Sometimes people remind me of those whom I have promised to remember. They tell me this is 'javelin' praying and I find it a wonderful way to keep in tune."

Another man prays early in the morning before breakfast. He goes to a particular chair in the balcony cove of his spacious home. He says this is a perfect start for his day. Here is a lady who prays after she gets in bed at night. She testifies that this is a great way to go to sleep. Here is a man who prays right after lunch in his office. He shuts his door and is "out" to the phone and to visitors until he has completed his quiet time with the Lord.

One lady says she runs through her group mentally each morning as she dresses. She names each one before God and asks him to give them to her as they need her prayers each day.

Here is an unusual idea. This man says, "My best praying is hooked up with my emotions. When I am blue I pray for my people and ask God to bless them when they're blue. If I'm worried, I pray for their worries. Most folks have fears, money problems, temper flashes. Do you think this is good? I feel sure it is and it does me good too."

This could go on and on. The fact is that there are limitless ranges waiting for your discovery in prayer. You work out your own system. Keep studying. Keep trying. And whatever feels right between you and God is all right with us. This is what we mean by "Pray in your own way."

In addition to presenting the varieties of possibilities, we have found that education for prayer must also place a strong emphasis on the difficulties involved. Whenever a believer comes out of the bleachers and gets into the game there are sure to be bumps and bruises. We make it clear to our workers that they have taken on a discipline which will be marked with personal disappointments and periods of dryness. Even our best praying members admit that there are days when they forget their assignments. Most of them state that they have what the mystics call "arid" expanses. But the grace of God is replete with second chances when the human heart is sincere. If the soul at prayer keeps asking God to make him more faithful, gradually he reaches break-through points where he feels he is making progress and is becoming more faithful in his covenant.

We also make it clear to our beginners that they may find this totally impossible for their service to the Kingdom. We place no shame on cessation of this work. There are countless other places to use one's talents in the life of the church. We make it possible for our prayer workers to resign their responsibilities gracefully and without embarrass-

107

ment. We only ask at the outset that they give a sincere try to making their church a "house of prayer" in keeping with the wish of the Master of prayer.

A phrase from Dietrich Bonhoeffer offers an appropriate word of conclusion. It is a statement which brings me to earth with a thud when I get impatient to bring in the Kingdom. With his usual incisive thrust he says, "We ought not to try and be more religious than God."

In the final analysis none but the divine mind knows what pace he has set for the total spiritual integration of his church. It seems to me that the great need of those of us who are anxious for a praying church is patience. We must not rush the sunrise nor hurry the rose to its blooming. Instead it is ours to plant seeds, lay foundations, start somewhere, and remember that the Lord is already at work. We are to furnish what tools we can, be alert to new openings, and remain diligent in our love for his plans for his people.

This is a good word for us from the apostle Paul: "The Lord direct your hearts into the love of God, and into the patient waiting for Christ." (II Thess. 3:5.)

Tested Bibliography

There are hundreds of excellent books on prayer which may be useful to prayer programs in the local church. We list here those which we have used in our work and found to be generally helpful to a majority of our people. It will be obvious to the discerning reader that many excellent volumes are not included. This is no reflection on the merit of the missing titles, but rather indicates that our groups have not yet had opportunity to put them into use. Also the list below does not include many fine little pieces which have been worked through by our Bible study units and other small groups.

The following are recommended by those who have studied them in their groups. Those marked with an asterisk have been especially adaptable in our youth groups.

Chambers, Oswald. *My Utmost for His Highest.* New York: Dodd, Mead & Co., 1956.

*Coburn, John B. *Prayer and Personal Religion.* Philadelphia: The Westminster Press, 1957.

Day, Albert Edward. *An Autobiography of Prayer.* New York: Harper & Row, Publishers, 1952.

Fenelon, Francois. *Christian Perfection.* Edited and prefaced by Charles F. Whiston; translated by Mildred Whitney Stillman. Harper & Row, Publishers, 1947. (Written in 1670.)

Fosdick, Harry Emerson. *The Meaning of Prayer.* Reflection book. New York: Association Press, 1962.

Freer, Harold W., and Hall, F. B. *Two or Three Together.* Harper and Row, Publishers, 1954.

Grou, Jean Nicolai. *How to Pray.* Translated by Joseph Dalley. New York: Harper and Row, Publisher, 1956.

Harkness, Georgia. *Prayer and the Common Life.* Apex edition. Nashville: Abingdon Press, 1962.

Kelly, Thomas R. *A Testament of Devotion.* New York: Harper and Row, Publishers, 1941.

Laubach, Frank C. *Prayer: The Mightiest Force in the World.* Westwood, N. J.: Fleming H. Revell Co., 1946.

Listen, the Lord. Santa Fe, N. M.: Rydall Press, 1956.

Lockyer, Herbert. *All the Prayers of the Bible.* Grand Rapids: Zondervan Publishing House, 1959.

Maclachlan, Lewis. *Common Sense About Prayer.* London: James Clarke & Co., Ltd., 1962.

―――――――. *How to Pray for Healing.* London: James Clarke & Co., Ltd., 1955.

―――――――. *Intelligent Prayer.* London: James Clarke & Co., Ltd., 1946.

―――――――. *Teachings of Jesus on Prayer.* London: James Clarke & Co., Ltd., 1952.

Murray, Andrew. *With Christ in the School of Prayer.* Westwood, N. J.: Fleming H. Revell Co., 1953.

*Shedd, Charlie and Martha. *Word Focusing: A New Way to Pray.* Nashville: The Upper Room Press, 1961.

Stewart, George S. *The Lower Levels of Prayer.* Nashville: Abingdon Press, 1940.

Underhill, Evelyn. *The Fruits of the Spirit, Light of Christ, and Abba: Meditations Based on the Lord's Prayer.* New York: David McKay Co., Inc., 1956.

In addition to books addressed strictly to the prayer theme, certain of our prayer study groups have found these helpful for their daily meditations and group studies:

Howe, Reuel. *Man's Need and God's Action.* Greenwich, Conn.: Seabury Press, Inc., 1953.

* Reynolds, Robert. *The Choice to Love.* New York: Harper and Rowe, Publishers, 1959.

Smith, Hannah. *The Christian's Secret of a Happy Life.* Westwood, N. J.: Fleming H. Revell, 1961.

*Weatherhead, Leslie. *The Will of God.* Nashville: Abingdon Press, 1944.

Two books which have been particularly helpful while discussing the setting up and conducting prayer study groups are:

Casteel, John L. *Spiritual Renewal Through Small Groups*. New York: Association Press, 1957.

Shoemaker, Helen Smith. *Power Through Prayer Groups: Their Why and How*. Westwood, N. J.: Fleming H. Revell, 1958.

An appendix of materials used in the prayer work described in this book is available from the author, #6 Sleepy Oaks, Houston, Texas 77024.

111